THE
POCKET SQUARE

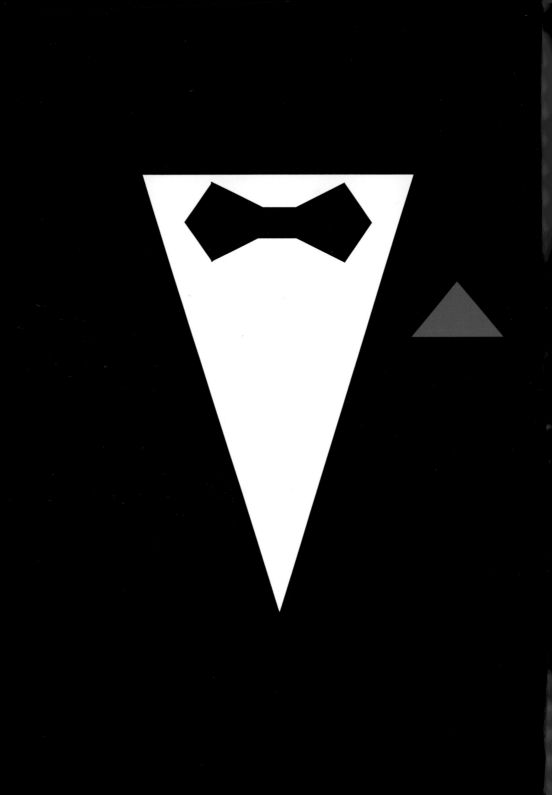

A. C. Phillips

THE
POCKET SQUARE

22 ESSENTIAL FOLDS

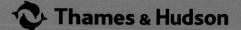

First published in 2016 in hardcover in the United States of America
by Thames & Hudson Inc., 500 Fifth Avenue, New York, New York 10110

thamesandhudsonusa.com

Library of Congress Control Number 2015953649

ISBN 978-0-500-51886-1

Printed and bound in China by C & C Offset Printing Co. Ltd

Contents

'One should either be a work of art, or wear a work of art.'

OSCAR WILDE

THE
POCKET SQUARE

T he pocket square has royal beginnings, with King Richard II of England inventing and popularizing handkerchiefs in the late 14th century: they first appear in his household roll of accounts as 'little pieces [of cloth] for the lord king to wipe and clean his nose.'

While handkerchiefs were originally used for hygiene, the demands of style and individuality soon led to square, round and even triangular forms, lavishly embroidered and fringed with lace.

By the end of the Renaissance, these 'little cloths' were commonplace throughout Western Europe, and becoming increasingly ornate. Fashion icon Marie Antoinette grew exasperated at the number of designs, and complained to her husband, King Louis XVI of France. He then published a decree that all handkerchiefs must have four sides of equal length, and they have remained square ever since.

At first, handkerchiefs were kept in trouser pockets. But as three- and two-piece suits came into fashion, jackets were cut with a left breast pocket, allowing them to be displayed.

Soon, the specific look of a handkerchief became key, and folding techniques came into fashion. The 'pocket square' shed its functional origins and became an accessory.

Having discovered the virtues of being well groomed, gentlemen would flaunt their squares, having one for show and one to blow. The pocket square and its fold permitted a rare sartorial opportunity for male self-expression.

Today, the square makes a stronger statement than ever, as gentlemen pay homage to a style that embraces the original workings of a suit. This collection, featuring details and designs from the golden age of folding to the present day, offers a range of options to explore and consider when executing a look.

There are as many ways to fold a pocket square as there are fabrics and designs to choose from: the art of folding ranges from the simple and austere to the complex and flamboyant.

Squares are generally made from silk, linen or cotton, and measure up to half a square metre. Folds tend to follow either a crease or puff method: due to their inherent stiffness, cotton and linen are suited to creases, while silk, being soft and flowing, is much better at forming puffs.

There are countless ways to display a square, but only a few are elegant. Like a signature, choose one that pleases you best and make it your mark.

'Clothes and manners
do not make the man;
but when he is made,
they greatly improve
his appearance.'

HENRY WARD BEECHER

The Folds

'Simplicity, to me,
has always been
the essence of
good taste.'

CARY GRANT

THE
TV

The TV fold with its consistent horizontal line is a fantastic way to show that a gentleman cares about his appearance beyond the minimum requirements.

Developed on Madison Avenue and popularized by television news presenters, today the fold's classic, understated elegance makes it the sartorial accent of choice for many men.

Expose a closed edge only, with the points folded inside. For a crisp presentation use a light poplin square to create sharp edges and tight creases.

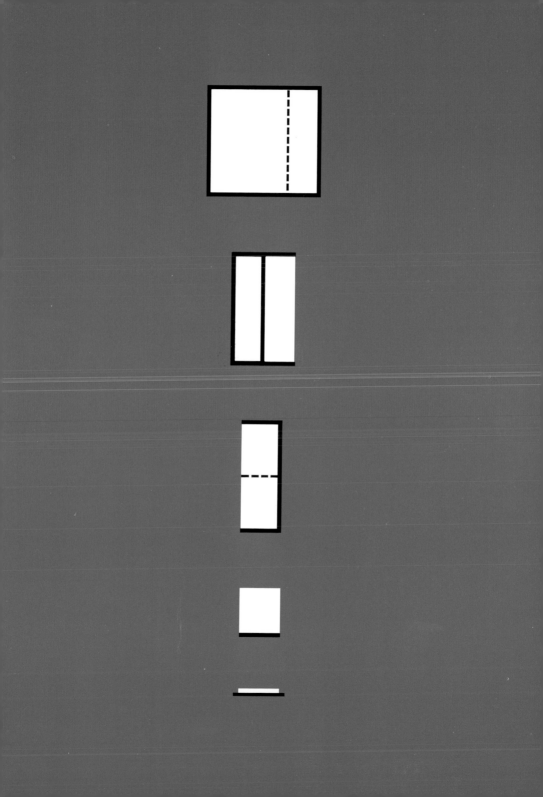

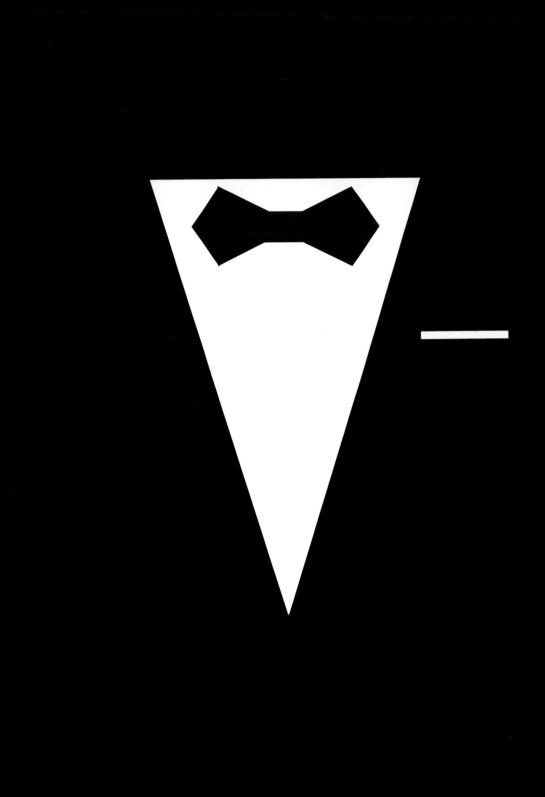

'You have to develop a style that suits you and pursue it, not just develop a bag of tricks.'

JAMES STEWART

THE
PRESIDENTIAL

The Presidential fold is the ultimate understatement, and perhaps the quickest way to elevate your style.

Acquiring its name while President Harry S Truman was in office, this is the simplest fold you can use to create a pulled-together yet not too business-like look.

Similar to the TV fold but with hand-finished edges showing at the top and right, the Presidential is a standard-issue pocket-square fold for everyday wear, adding a finishing touch to comfortable elegance.

For larger squares it may be necessary to use an extra side or bottom fold. Adjust to display only a sliver of white.

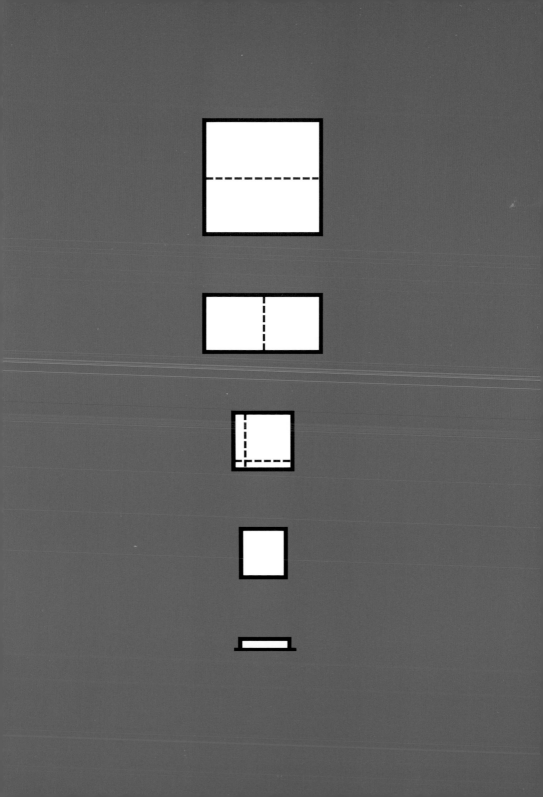

'His tastes were very traditional, but he was attuned to the young too. I was just a twenty-year-old, starstruck kid at the time, but I remember that Kennedy would ask me what fabrics I liked.'

PAUL WINSTON — CHIPP CLOTHIERS

THE
PEAK

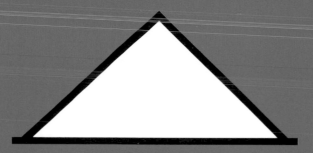

JFK was the Peak's biggest proponent, whether worn in his Ivy League, Brooks Brothers days as part of his signature East Coast style or during his presidential collaboration with his tailors, Sidney Winston at Chipp and Sam Harris.

He nearly always sported the fold, albeit with a very low point, as his reading glasses would crush the Peak throughout the day.

Ensure you place the square in your pocket with the folds at the back and the point at the front to create a more pronounced look. Wear the Peak high, with confidence and panache!

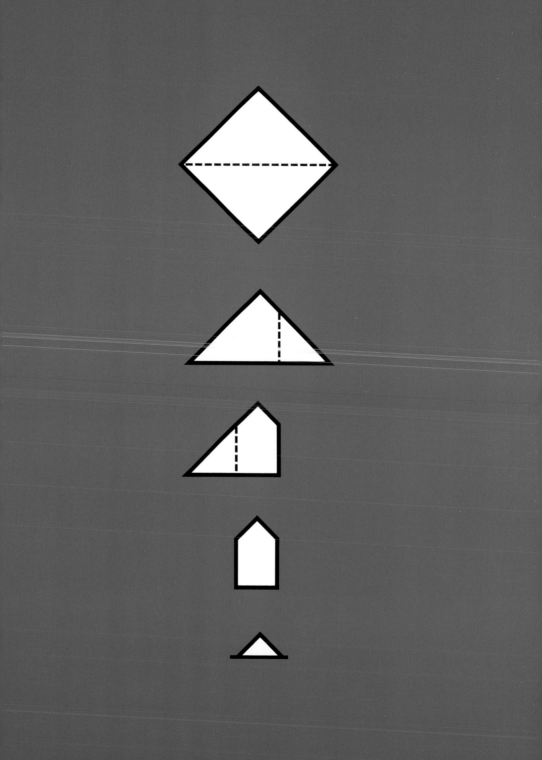

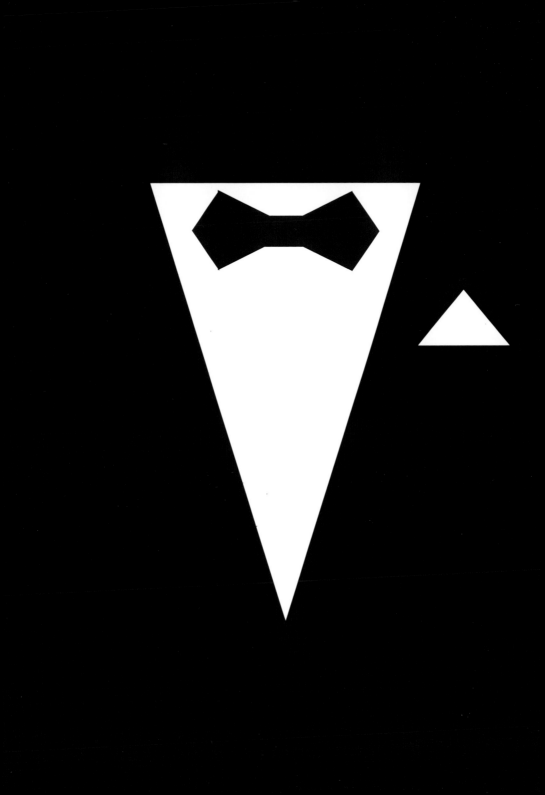

'To achieve the nonchalance which is absolutely necessary for a man, one article at least must not match.'

HARDY AMIES

THE
TWO POINT

Similar to the Peak, the Two Point is a classic. It was popularized by Sir Edwin Hardy Amies, court dressmaker to Queen Elizabeth II.

The Two Point is suitable for all square types. Ensure the points are constructed from a creased edge instead of the open ends, as this will make them much stronger.

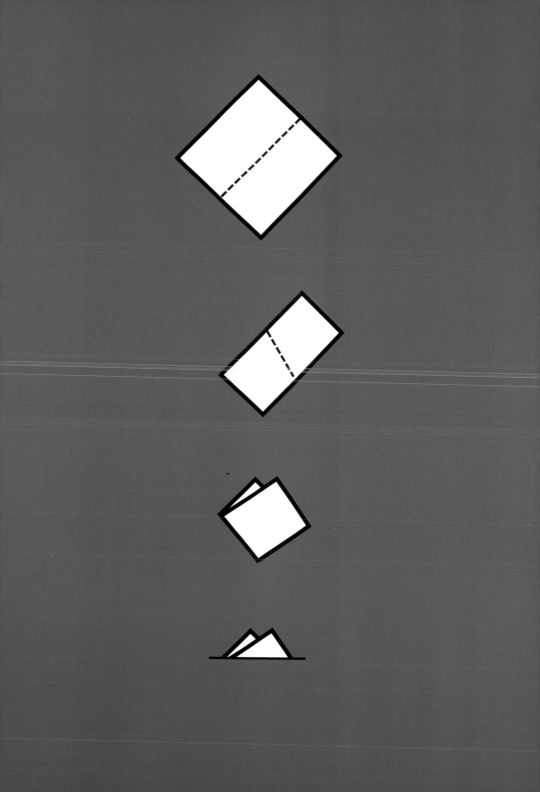

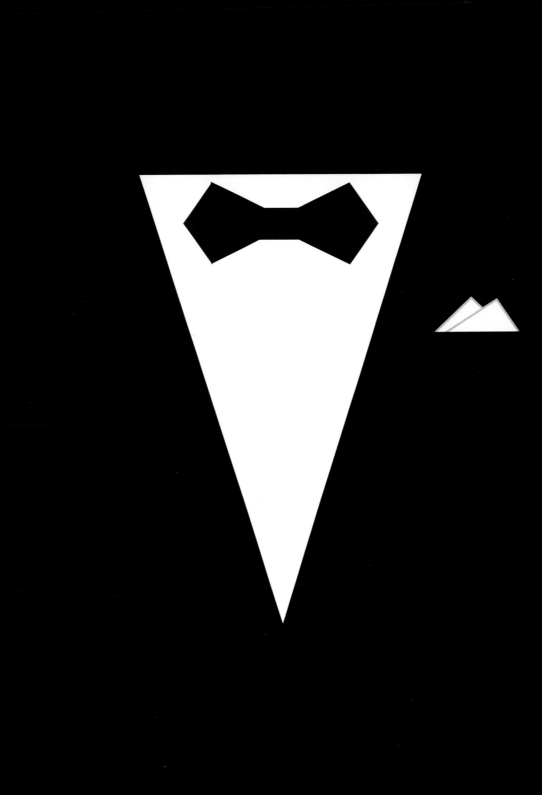

'Dress up your sportswear and dress down your formal wear.'

LUCIANO BARBERA

THE
TULIP

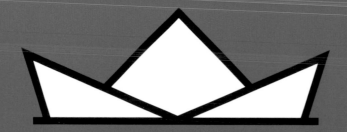

The Tulip is a sharp and pointy number, excellent with cotton and linen squares. The elegant triangular effect is perfectly suited to sporty blazers, creating a rakish, contemporary look.

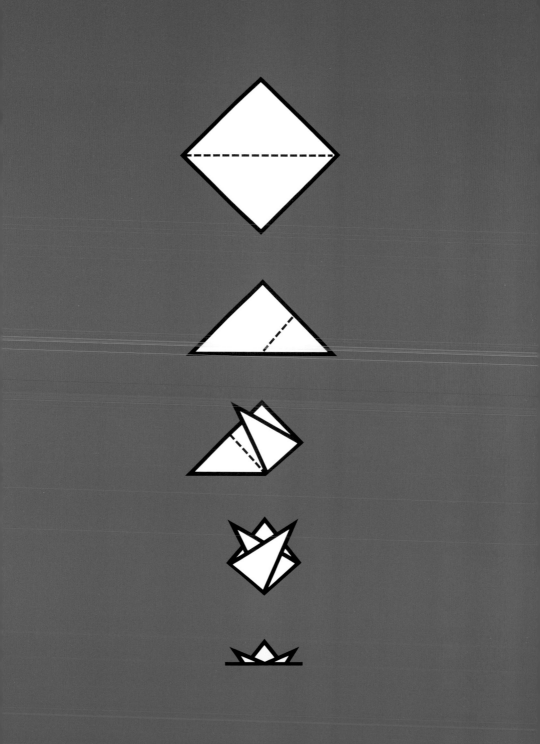

'Pocket
handkerchiefs
are optional, but
I always wear one.'

FRANK SINATRA

THE
FOUR POINT

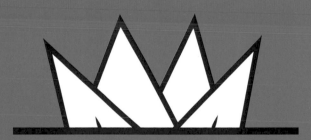

The Four Point is the most convivial of accoutrements, well suited to the bon vivant in a rush.

Pinch to form a puff before stuffing the little cloud into the base of your pocket. Tease the points to create the desired effect.

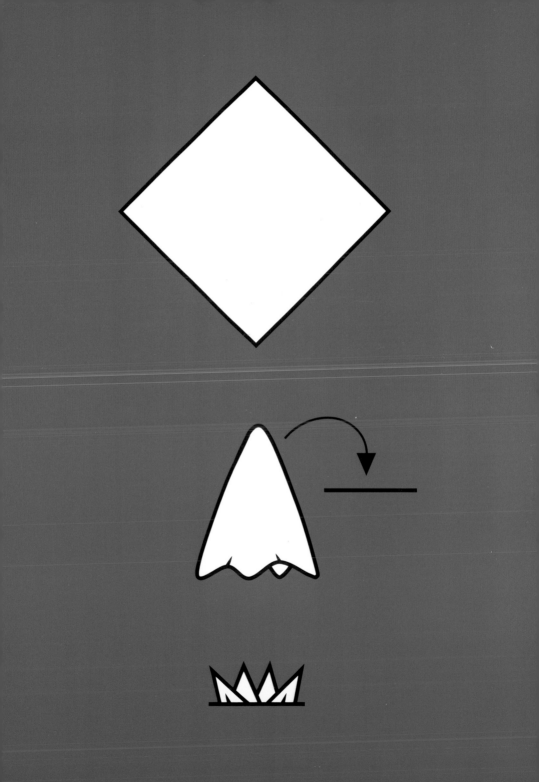

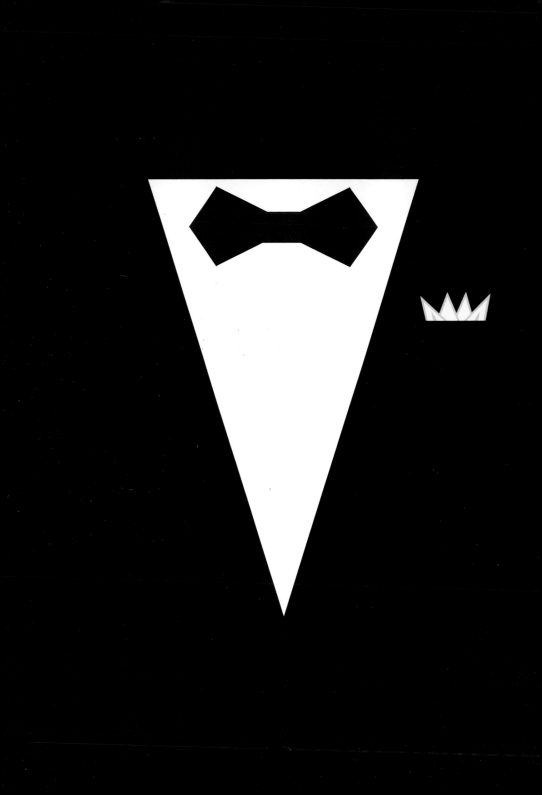

'Style is knowing
who you are, what
you want to say, and
not giving a damn.'

GORE VIDAL

THE
CRUISELINER

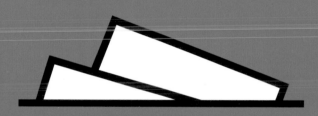

Pull up a deckchair and relax in style. The Cruiseliner's raked-bow-and-chimney-stack combination creates a beautiful silhouette against a pocket's gentle slope.

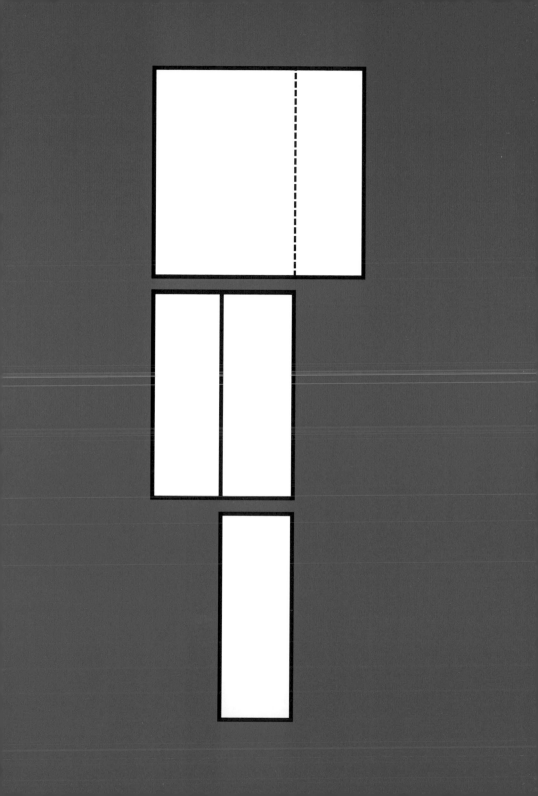

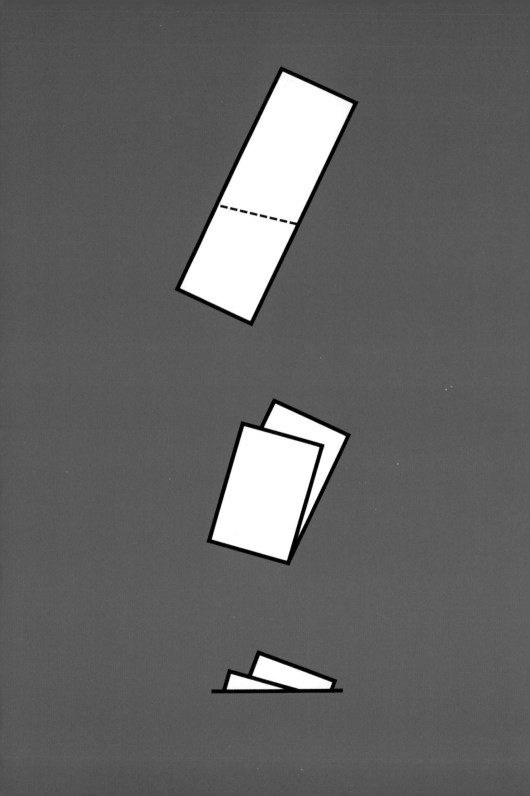

'You don't find a style. A style finds you.'

KEITH RICHARDS

'Live fast, die
young, and leave a
good-looking corpse.'

WILLARD MOTLEY

THE
CAGNEY

Some gentlemen may wish to define themselves by sporting a more elaborate, indulgent fold, and no fold is more elaborate and indulgent than the Cagney, named after the legend of film and Broadway James Cagney.

This favourite has all four points on show: two in the centre, slightly offset, framed by one either side.

The Cagney's multiple peaks create a very elaborate style, and are a great complement to the tailored splendour of a three-piece suit.

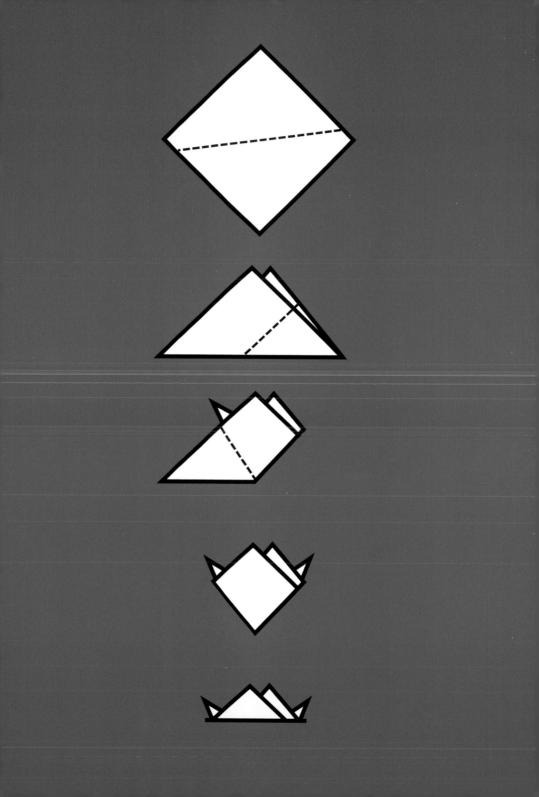

'Looking good and dressing well is a necessity. Having a purpose in life is not.'

OSCAR WILDE

FOUR OF A KIND

Four of a Kind is a much tighter variation on the Cagney. For this heavily lined design, try using a shoestring square. Its contrasting border highlights the fold's carefully choreographed lines while enhancing the movement of the lapel.

Fold the square into offset quarters, creating four evenly spaced points. The open ends should fan out at the top like a hand of playing cards. Tweak to fit, with each point aimed at your shoulder.

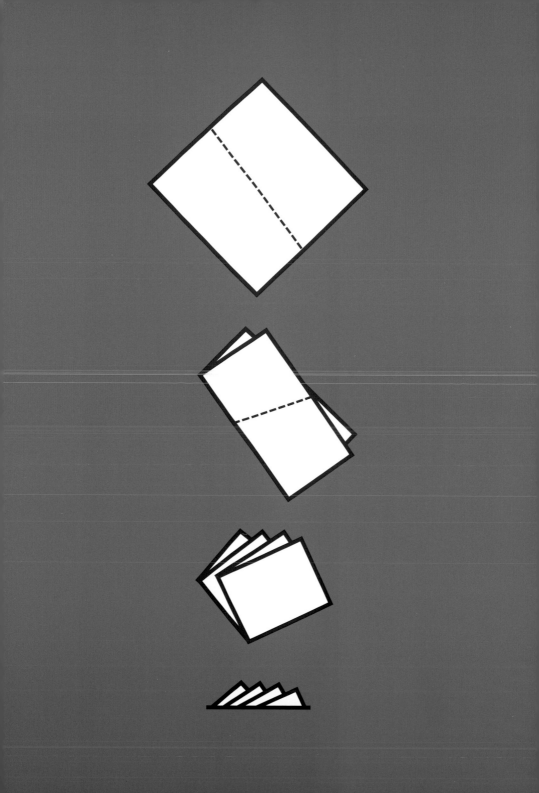

'One pretends to do something, or copy someone or some teacher, until it can be done confidently and easily in what becomes one's own style.'

CARY GRANT

DIAMONDS
ARE FOREVER

This beautiful fold creates intense, arresting lines through a stack of diamond points. The extra sheeting from the number of layers also creates a strong, pocket-centred look.

Some pocket-square aficionados may choose to combine two squares for extra padding. This also enables the wearer to carry one for show and one to blow!

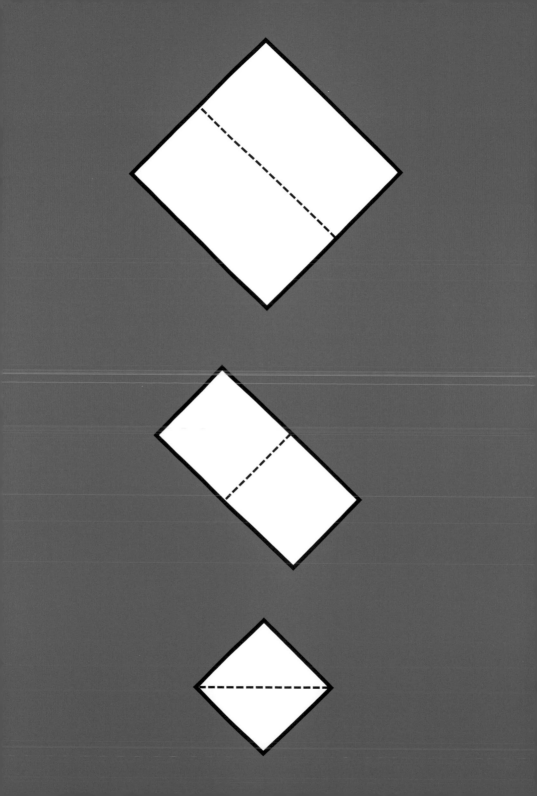

'Isn't elegance forgetting what one is wearing?'

YVES SAINT LAURENT

LE
CROISSANT

Le Croissant is a display of taste and creativity. With its heavily creased pattern, this elegant *muchoir de poche* will satisfy the origami expert who yearns for a unique, attention-grabbing design.

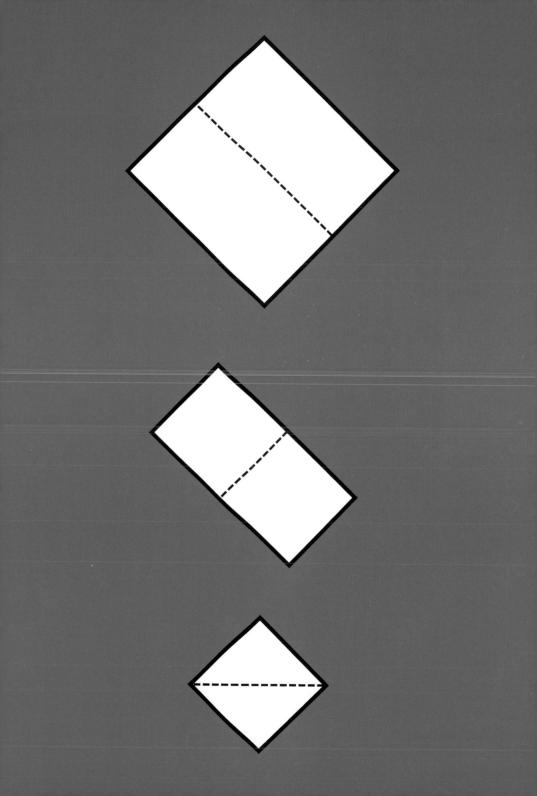

'Style is a simple way of saying complicated things.'

JEAN COCTEAU

THE
TAIL FIN

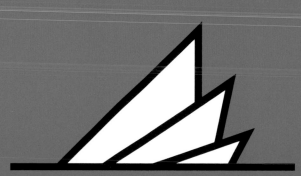

With its air of brash formality, this prickly three-fin design should be angled jauntily away from the heart, accentuating the V of a suit while broadening the shoulders.

For an individualistic twist, the actor Cary Grant famously wore his pointing inwards, clashing the angle of his square with the movement of the lapel.

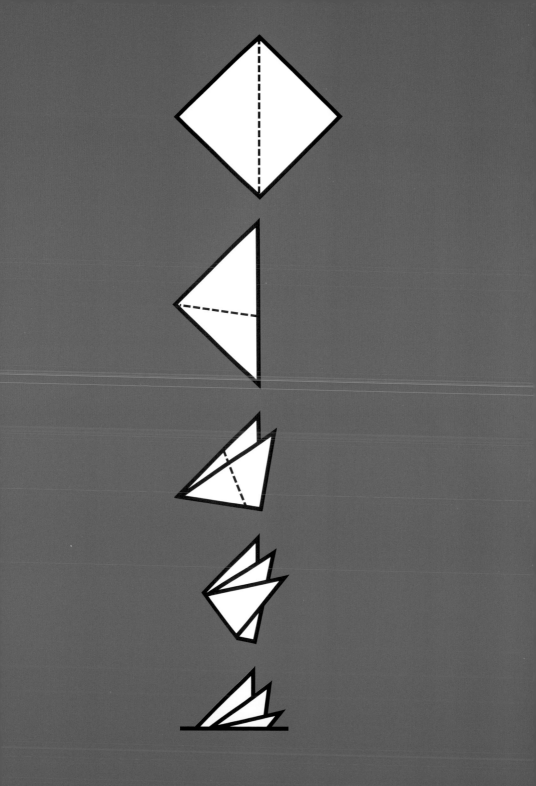

'A man should look as
if he had bought his clothes
with intelligence, put them
on with care, and then
forgotten all about them.'

HARDY AMIES

THE
DIAGONAL
SHELL

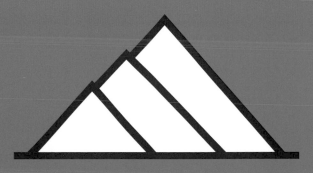

The Diagonal Shell is a disarmingly beautiful, pleated fold that takes surprisingly little time to execute. The gorgeous shells should be staggered upwards to the left.

A thickly woven linen or cotton square works best. And remember not to play with it – you will lose those lovely crisp lines!

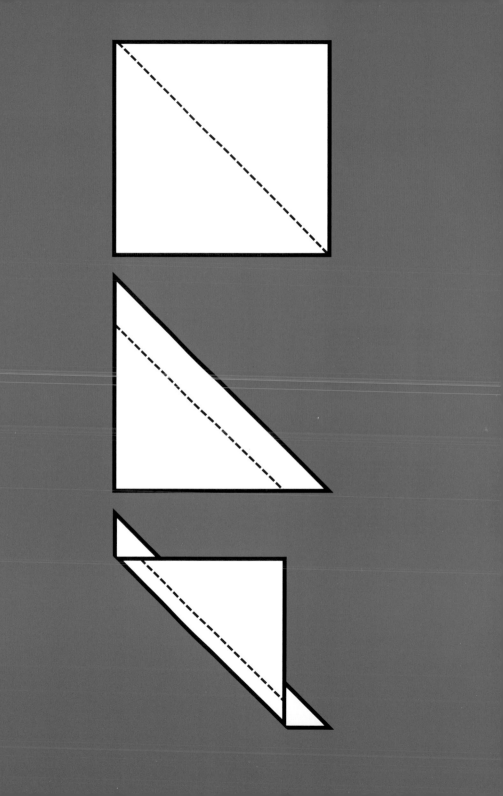

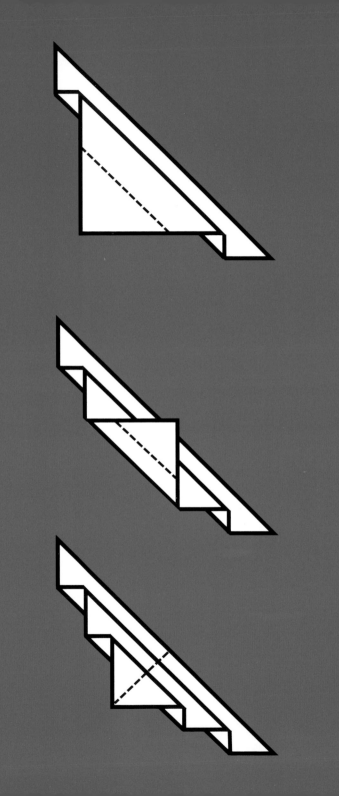

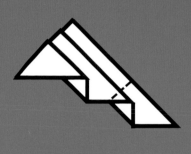

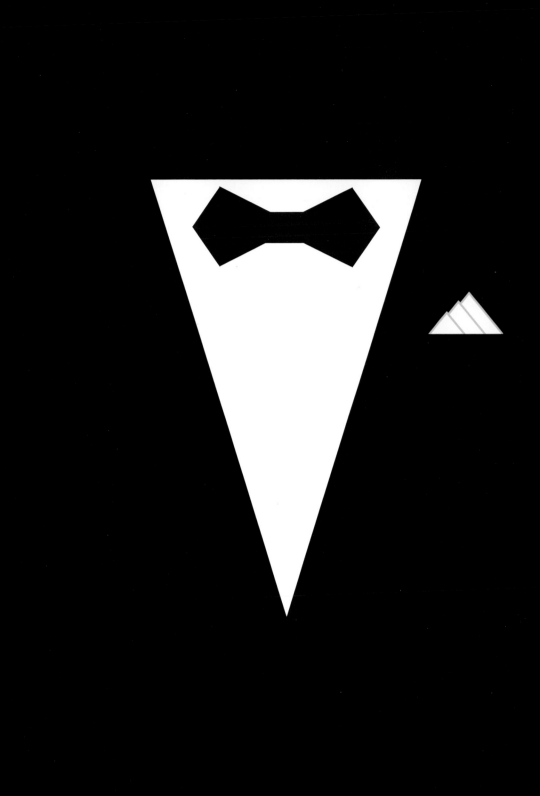

'I was in fact produced as a leader of fashion, with the clothiers as my showmen and the world as my audience.'

THE DUKE OF WINDSOR

THE
WINDSOR
PUFF

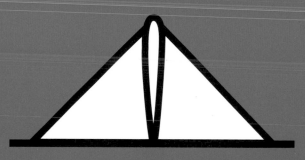

The Windsor Puff, with its gently curved wing, embodied the duke's fondness for the soft silhouettes of English drapery.

One of the simplest and yet most distinctive folds, it is equally well suited to cotton or silk squares. Fold the square into quarters before pulling down two corners to form a hooded crease.

Consider adding other accoutrements, such as a cravat or floral boutonnière, to put a finishing touch to this aristocratic ensemble.

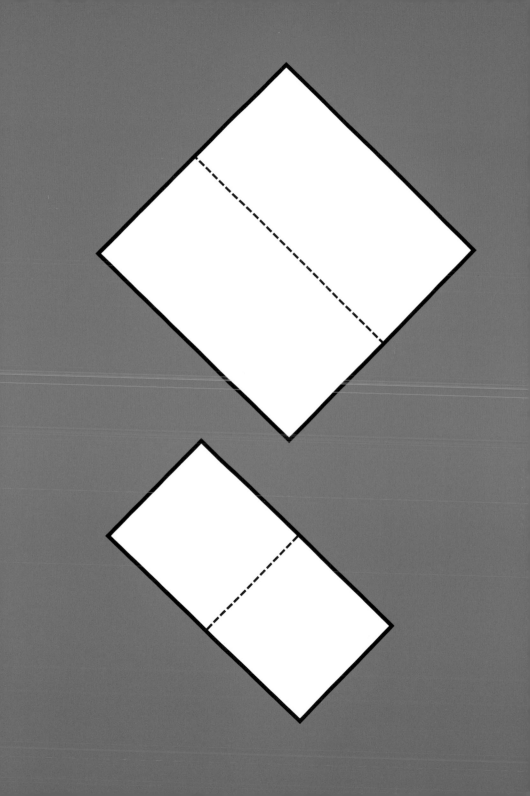

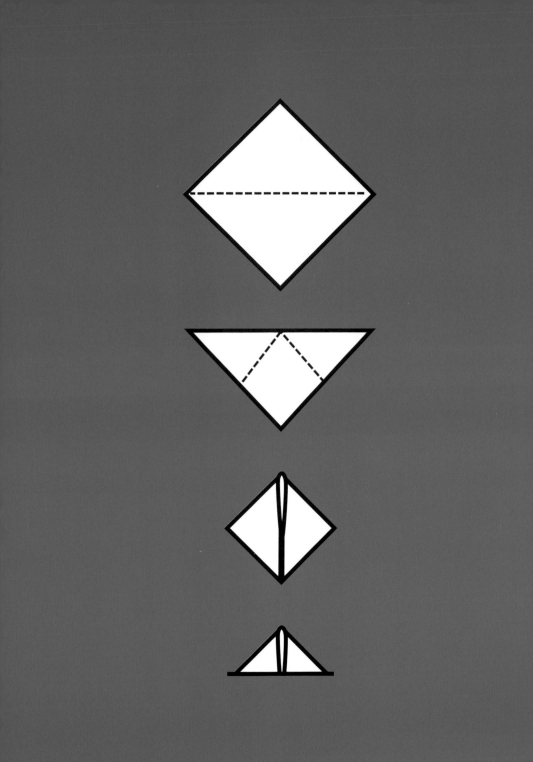

'Looking good isn't self-importance; it's self-respect.'

CHARLES HIX

'I figured you had to sort of be their ideal. I don't mean a handsome knight riding a white horse, but a fella who answered the description of a right guy.'

GARY COOPER

THE
COOPER PUFF

G

Gary Cooper received a number of Academy Awards for playing tough guys. When he put on a suit, however, he never forgot the delicate little details. In fact, he even had this billowy fold named after him.

The debonair Cooper Puff brings a touch of ceremony to a pocket, creating a polished look. Puffs shouldn't be rigid, so silk squares, with their floaty lightness and pillowy texture, are ideal.

Pinch the centre and draw the square upwards, with all four points facing down. Fill your pocket with the points to create a base for your little cloud. Shape to add fullness – a voluminous puff is best!

For a more floral look, consider a shibori square. This Japanese art form involves dyeing fabric to create intricate, often flower-like patterns.

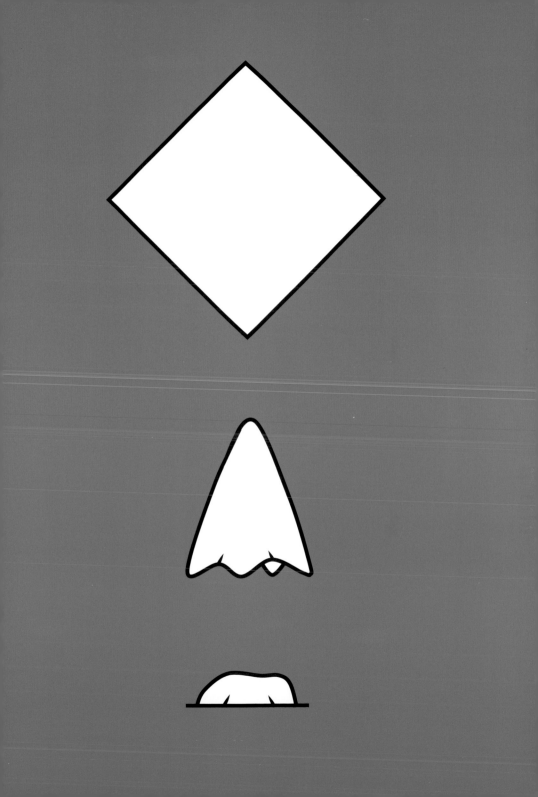

'A man must face the
world with sprezzatura.
It literally means detachment,
but a better way to think of it
is quiet confidence or low-
key style. The most forceful
statement is understatement.'

LUCIANO BARBERA

THE
GUIDO PUFF

Grab your *fazzoletto* to create this variation on the Cooper Puff. Discovered by a distinguished Italian *signore* in a famous scarf shop, the Guido Puff is a beautiful fold that achieves the elusive Italian quality of 'sprezzatura' – studied carelessness.

Carefully lift a small puff from each corner – as well as from the middle – to display the loose crumple of your five-puff fold. As a subtle sartorial gesture, ensure no corners or edges show.

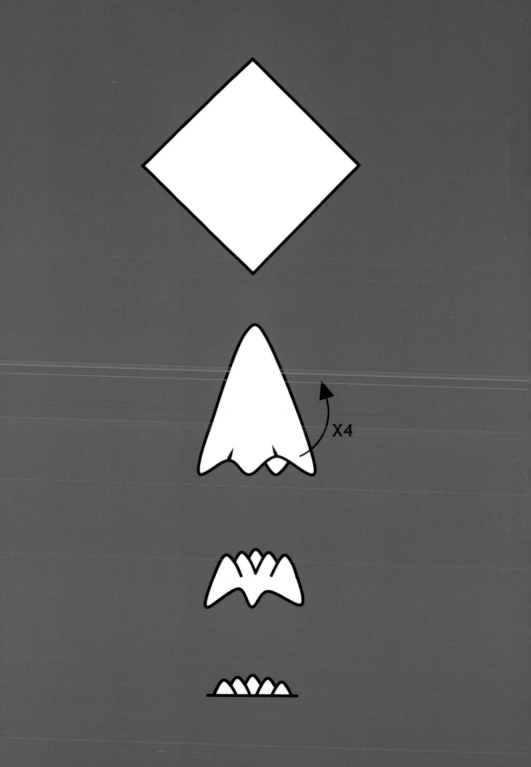

X4

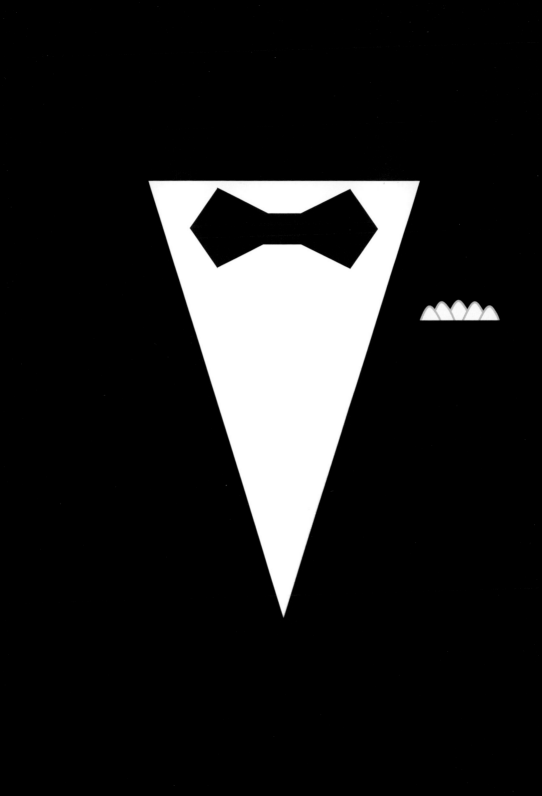

'I often take a brand-new suit or hat and throw it up against the wall a few times to get that stiff, square newness out of it.'

FRED ASTAIRE

THE
FRED ASTAIRE

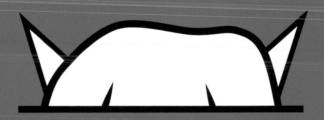

The grand old stars of the silver screen heavily influenced pocket squares. Fred Astaire, known for his flowing style, was rarely photographed without one, and even invented his very own fold.

Casually executed, this dapper fold is simply a Cooper Puff gathered with a point peeking out on either side. Stuff it with style!

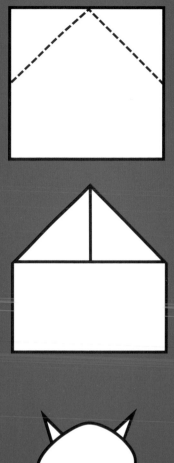

'To improve is to change, so to be perfect is to have changed often.'

WINSTON CHURCHILL

THE
ROLLED PUFF

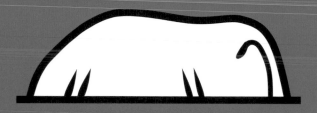

An alternative fold to the Cooper Puff is the similar but much more textured Rolled Puff. Wind a puff down to create large rolls, until you run out of material.

Like all squares, the effect of a Rolled Puff can be terrific. Sir Winston Churchill wore a huge number of pocket-square designs and variants to project his image as an orator. For some of his finest speeches he would tease two twisted points from the sides of his Rolled Puff to create a striking 'V for Victory'.

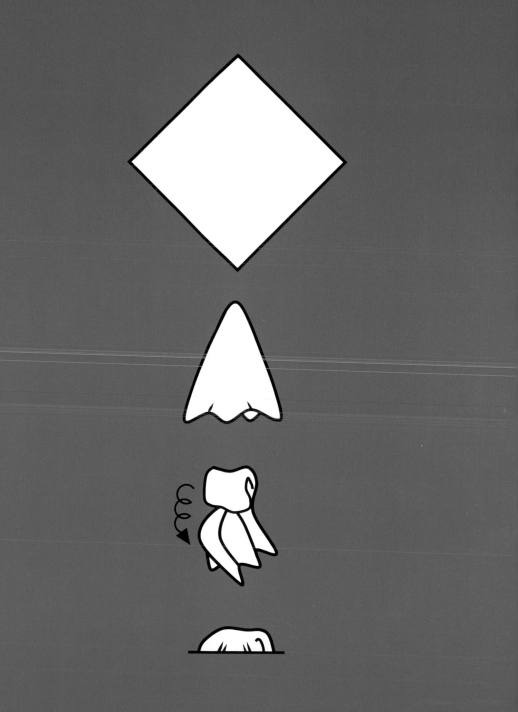

'The impulse towards perfection is more important than perfection itself.'

FAYE DUNAWAY

THE
DUNAWAY

Shrouded in mystery, this fold relates to the seduction of Faye Dunaway's character in *The Thomas Crown Affair.*

With a light-pink striped shirt, lilac necktie and black-and-silver pocket-square combination, Steve McQueen epitomized the 1960s 'Peacock Revolution'. Menswear shifted from plain, dark tailoring to a riot of colour, with boots, frills and cravats clashing with collarless jackets and wide, exaggerated lapels.

The Dunaway is an equally elaborate combination of four teased points and a heavily rolled puff.

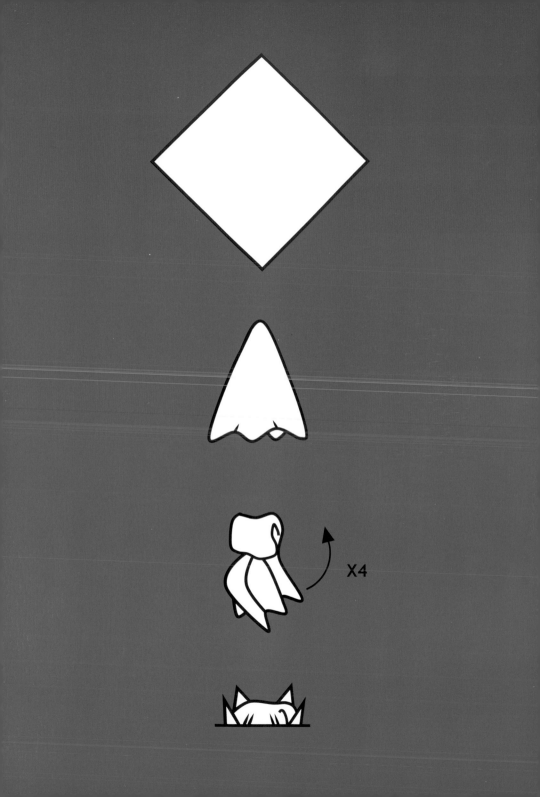

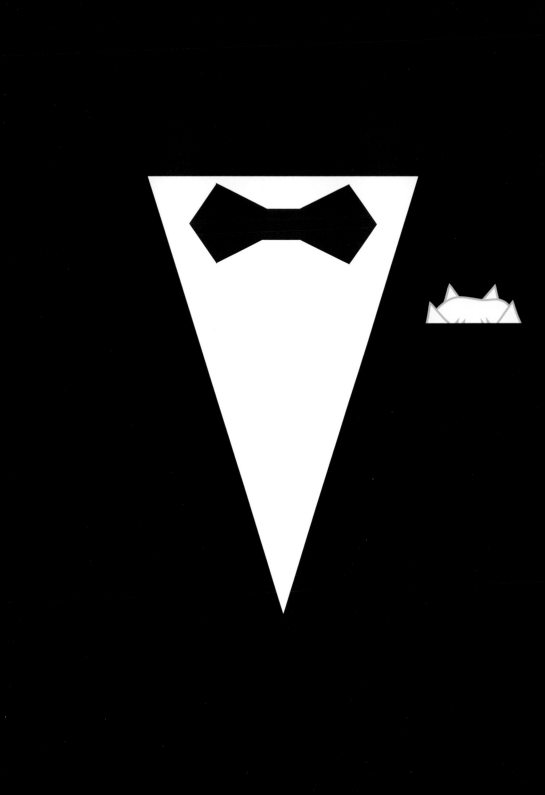

'Forget about being correct
and being exact. It's just
a charming accessory.
It adds beauty, colour
and movement so it
should not follow a rule.'

JEAN-CLAUDE COLBAN

THE
BOUQUET

A dramatic, showy fold, the Bouquet should burst from your pocket. For a more textural look, consider using a pocket round, with its elegant furled edge.

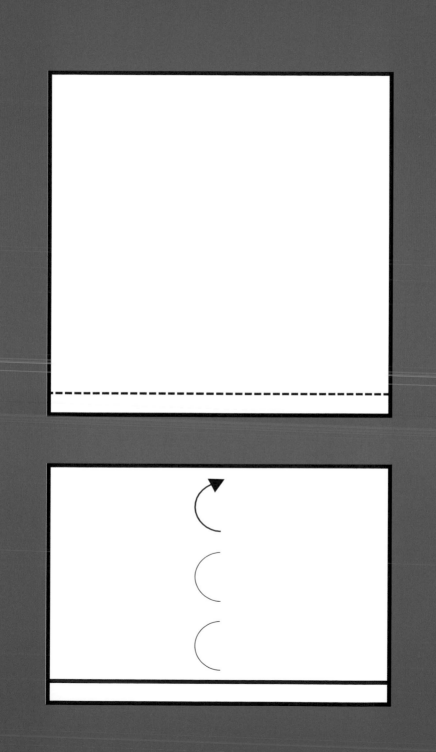

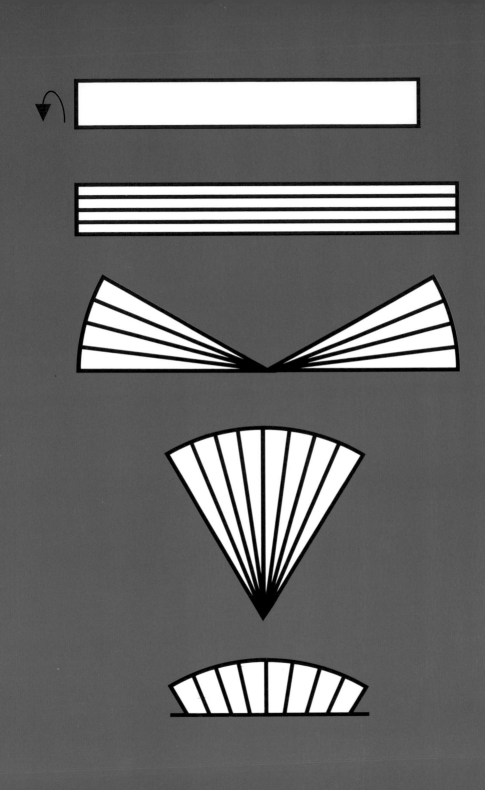

'Dressing well is a form of good manners.'

TOM FORD

'Can't repeat the past? Why of course you can!'

JAY GATSBY

THE
CARROT

ooking for a 1920s Jazz-era fold straight out of an F Scott Fitzgerald novel? The Carrot – uber rare, retro and damn showy – is made to be worn to flapper-girl parties.

Gather three corners and drape the square into a kinked Z-shape, with the seat tucked in and three points sprouting up. Use a large silk or vintage square, perhaps with lace detailing that speaks of another age.

Boho and rascally, if you can pull this off you are a dandy who can wear anything. How about a pair of red tartan trousers, braces and a pipe or monocle to match?

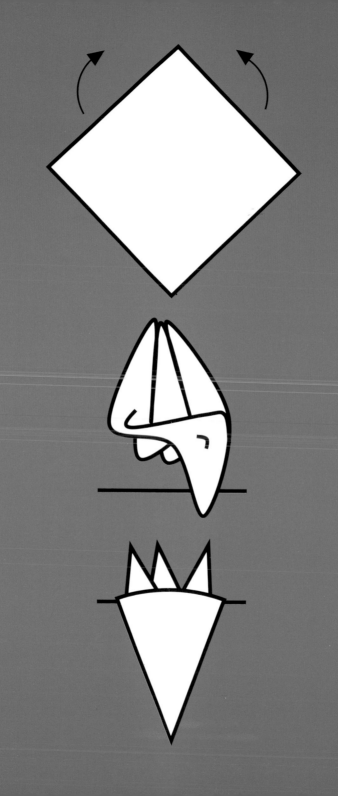

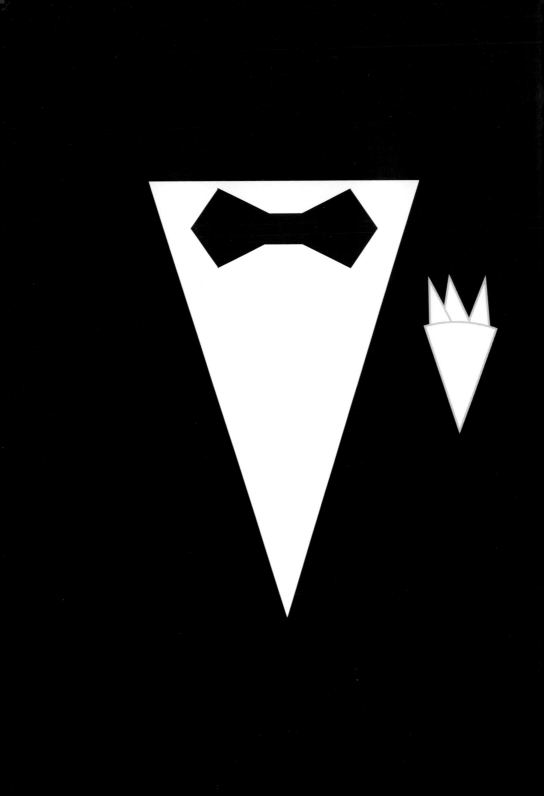

'Good clothes
open all doors.'

THOMAS FULLER

THE
VESPER

There are many Martinis, but there is only one Vesper Martini. It was invented by Ian Fleming's alter ego, Agent 007.

The Vesper fold's triangular Martini-glass pattern should be worn with a dark lounge suit to poker tables and cocktail bars.

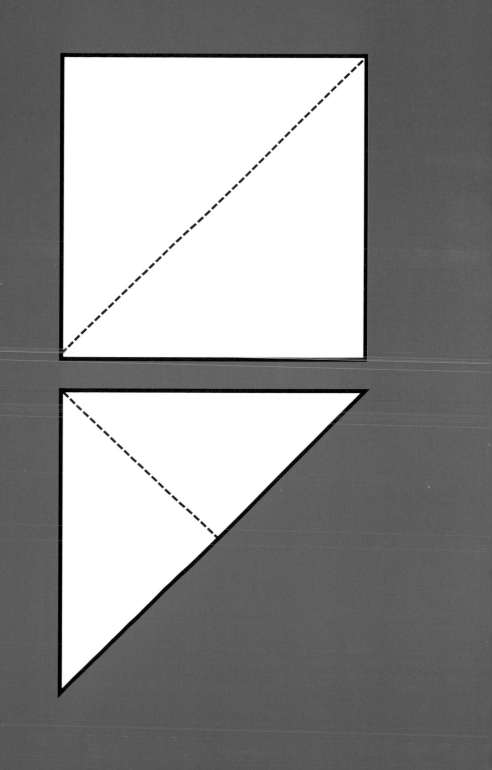

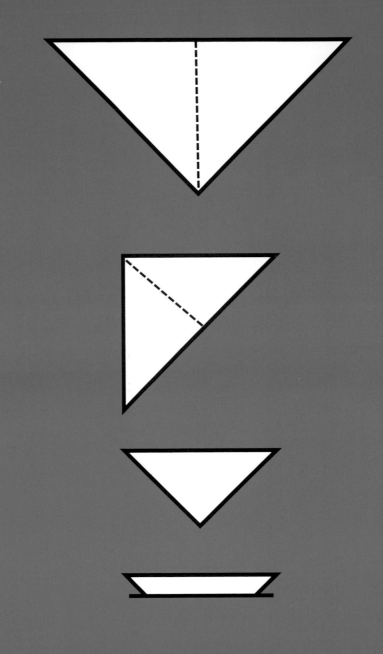

'The style of studied nonchalance is the psychological triumph of grace over order.'

G. BRUCE BOYER

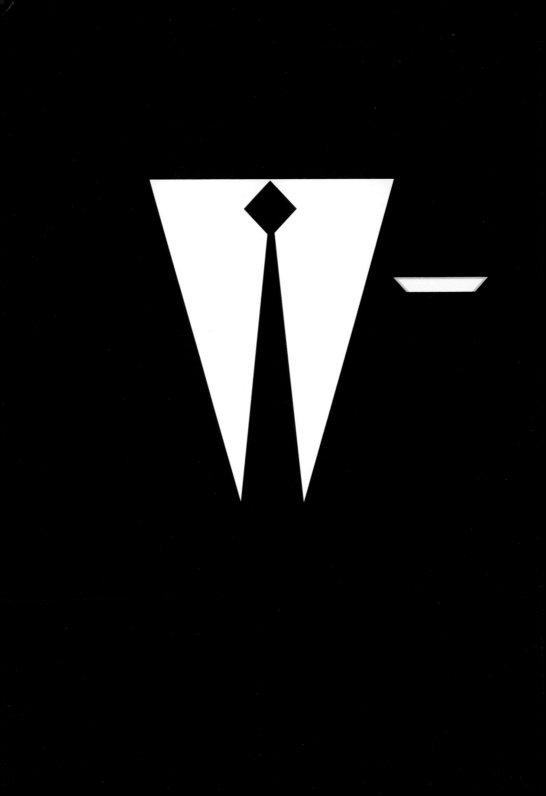

HOW TO WEAR A SQUARE

—

A gentleman will not only match a pocket square with his look but tastefully contrast it to act as a complementary accent.

There are no set rules when it comes to choosing a square. Any fabric can be used. Textural difference – the weave, weight and thickness of a fabric – is perhaps the most important consideration; it is why silk creates such a different impression to that of linen or cotton.

If you are wearing a dark, heavy wool or tweed suit and your tie is cotton or worsted, then a silk or poplin square may be a good option. If your suit is smooth and you are wearing a silk tie, adding another glossy fabric to this sleek ensemble may be excessive. Instead, opt for a textured linen or heavy cotton Oxford, twill or herringbone design. No tie? Then anything goes.

A pocket square can bring casual elegance to a look without a necktie.

Matching colours too closely, particularly those in the tie, can look monochromatic. Instead, choose a secondary colour from the suit or shirt to create a coordinated look. If you lack confidence mixing colours and designs then dress conservatively: white is never wrong, and complements any colour.

Patterns should be varied as the mood dictates. Paisley, bandana, gingham and polka-dot designs are busy, bold and fun. Plain, clean block colours, on the other hand, are classic and subtle.

For weddings and morning suits, whites, ivories, pinks and golds all work. A wedding is also one of the few occasions when it is appropriate to wear a tie similar to the square.

If it is after six, then you will be wearing a black or blue dinner jacket. This merits a red, white or ivory dress square made from linen or silk. A white dinner jacket may be more limiting, but a black-square-and-red-boutonnière combination is always stunning.

It may be desirable to tailor a fold to the cut of a suit. Two- and three-button jackets with slim notch lapels require an understated look, whereas the casual elegance of a sports jacket or blazer balances any fold. Strongly roped single buttons, double-breasted jackets and large peak lapels demand a brasher style.

Inject your square with character and individuality, making a statement about yourself and your mission. As with a hat, however, wear it with a degree of nonchalance, as if a square's only mission in life were to mop up spilled champagne from a lady's dress.

ETIQUETTE

—

1

Match your pocket square with your shirt, shoes, socks,
belt, hat, gloves or trousers. But not your tie!

2

Unlike a tie, it is always appropriate to wear a pocket square. If a gentleman is
wearing a jacket with an open pocket, it should have a square in it! Without one, the
pocket is an unnecessary detail and the jacket appears undressed.

3

Boutonnières and lapel flowers should not be worn on, in or near a pocket and its
square. Instead, pin or thread them through the lapel buttonhole.

4

Buy the finest squares your budget allows. They should have tight, hand-rolled edges
with hidden, regularly spaced stitches. Avoid flat or machine-hemmed edges.

5

Pocket squares should always be scrupulously spotless and only ever dry-cleaned.
Wearing cologne on your square will discolour and ruin its fabric.

6

For the love of fashion, avoid jackets with sewn-in squares. Don't pin, starch or fold
squares around stiffeners either. For sharp, fixed lines, fold and iron firmly. Silk
should be pressed lightly under cotton.

7

A gentleman should carry one square for show and another to blow, the latter living in
your hip or inside-jacket pocket. A white cotton or linen square may be removed and
used as a handkerchief; however, after using it you may never return it to the pocket
from whence it came. Silk squares cannot be used in this manner.

8

High pocket squares show extreme bravado. The old rule of having just an inch on
show no longer holds. However, simultaneously displaying a lot of shirt cuff may
detract from your overall look.

9

Monogrammed handkerchiefs? A discreet monogram can be fun
and personal, but heavy advertising is ostentatious and fussy.

10

Never leave your pocket square in a hanging jacket.
Remove and store it safely in a TV fold.

11

The controversy of the outer coat! A square does not belong in an outer-coat
pocket. If you feel the need, place a pipe or a nice pair of leather gloves in there
(fingers pointing out, of course). Equally, cigarettes, business cards, sunglasses and
stationery should not be stored in your jacket pocket. Squares only!

12

Never place a square in a waistcoat or shirt pocket. Shirts with pockets
should be linen, long-sleeved and for summer outfits. The pocket should
be used to house sunglasses.

13

A pocket square can be any size. But it should never be confused with its
rectangular cousin, the napkin. Every sartorialist should experiment with
different shapes, fabrics and designs, including rounds, triangles, bordered
shoestring designs and other clothiers' inventions.

14

Building your own signature fold through trial and error can be fun,
and over time one gains a sense of what works best. Keep them simple, though;
the placing of the handkerchief should not seem overly studied or complex.